WW kitchen collection

Sweet

Spring gift idea
Coconut ice bars, page 36

Autumn afternoon tea with friends
Carrot cake with cream cheese frosting, page 48

Summertime easy dessert
Cherry meringue pies, page 100

Winter warmer pud
Quickie fruit crumble, page 78

Sweet

The small print

EGGS We use medium eggs, unless otherwise stated. Pregnant women, the elderly and children should avoid recipes with eggs which are not fully cooked or raw.

FRUIT AND VEGETABLES Recipes use medium-sized fruit and veg, unless otherwise stated.

REDUCED FAT SOFT CHEESE Where a recipe uses reduced fat soft cheese, we mean a soft cheese with 25% less fat than its full fat equivalent.

LOW FAT SPREAD When a recipe uses a low fat spread, we mean a spread with a fat content of no less than 38%.

MICROWAVES If we have used a microwave in any of our recipes, the timings will be for an 850 watt microwave oven.

PREP AND COOKING TIMES These are approximate and meant to be guidelines. Prep time includes all the steps up to and following the main cooking time(s). Cooking times may vary according to your oven.

GLUTEN FREE The use of the term 'gluten free' or the 'gluten free icon' is illustrative only. Weight Watchers is not responsible for the presence of gluten in the dishes that have not been prepared in accordance with instructions; nor is it responsible for gluten contamination due to an external cause. Recipes labelled as gluten free, or displaying the gluten free icon, only include ingredients that naturally do not contain gluten. Whenever using canned, bottled or other types of packaged processed ingredients, such as sauces and stocks, it is essential to check that those ingredients do not contain gluten.

SmartPoints have been calculated using the values for generic foods, not brands (except where stated). Tracking using branded items may affect the recorded SmartPoints.

Seven.

Produced by Seven Publishing on behalf of Weight Watchers International, Inc. Published June 2016. All rights reserved. No part of this publication may be reproduced, stored in a retrieval system or transmitted in any form by any means, electronic, mechanical photocopying, recording or otherwise, without the prior written permission of Seven Publishing.

First published in Great Britain by Seven Publishing Ltd. Copyright © 2016, Weight Watchers International, Inc.

Seven Publishing Ltd
3-7 Herbal Hill
London
EC1R 5EJ
www.seven.co.uk

This book is copyright under the Berne Convention. No reproduction without permission. All rights reserved.

10 9 8 7 6 5 4 3 2 1

Weight Watchers SmartPoints and the SmartPoints icon are the registered trademarks of Weight Watchers International, Inc and are used under license by Weight Watchers (UK) Ltd. All rights reserved.

A CIP catalogue record for this book is available from the British Library. ISBN: 978-0-9935835-1-3

WEIGHT WATCHERS PUBLICATIONS TEAM Imogen Prescott, Samantha Rees, Nicola Kirk, Stephanie Williams, Danielle Smith.

PHOTOGRAPHY Steve Baxter, Tony Briscoe, Ian Garlick, Jonathan Kennedy, Neale Haynes, Lauren Mclean, Ria Osborne, Stuart Ovenden, Holly Pickering, William Shaw, Sam Stowell

RECIPES & FOOD STYLING Sarah Akhurst, Sue Ashworth, Lorna Brash, Linzi Brechin, Nadine Brown, Tamsin Burnett-Hall, Kate Calder, Gabriella English, Nicola Graimes, Alexis Grant, Catherine Hill, Jennifer Joyce, Laura Kettle, Jenna Leiter, Jennie Milsom, Kim Morphew, Mima Sinclair, Vicki Smallwood, Christine Stephens, Penny Stephens, Sarah Varney, Polly Webb-Wilson, Hannah Yeadon

PROP STYLING Linda Berlin, Emily Blunden, Liz Hippisley, Tony Hutchinson, Jenny Iggleden, Rachel Jukes, Joanna Levitas, Heather Matthews, Luis Peral, Zoe Regoczy, Olivia Wardle, Tamsin Weston, Holly White

FOR SEVEN PUBLISHING LTD

EDITORIAL & DESIGN
Editor-in-Chief Helen Renshaw, **Editor** Ward Hellewell
Art director Liz Baird, **Picture editor** Carl Palmer

ACCOUNT MANAGEMENT
Account manager Jo Brennan, **Business Director, retail** Andy Roughton, **Group publishing director** Kirsten Price

PRODUCTION
Production director Sophie Dillon
Colour reproduction by F1 Colour **Printed in Italy** by L.E.G.O S.p.A

Contents

We all fancy something sweet

every now and then, and one of the great things about Weight Watchers is that no food is forbidden. So while most of us know that **when it comes to sugar, less is best**, it's definitely still possible to have your cake and eat it too!

This book brings together some of the most popular recipes from the Weight Watchers kitchen — recipes you can make and enjoy, knowing exactly what's gone into them. Some are **lower in sugar**, while others use **sugar substitutes** or other **sweet ingredients** that still taste amazing. Some are **special-occasion treats**, but most can be enjoyed more often — there's even a zero SmartPoints recipe you can eat whenever you like.

From **sweet snacks** such as biscuits, brownies, traybakes and scones, to irresistible cakes and hot and cold puddings, you'll find plenty to choose from in this collection. Each recipe has been tried and tested, and we've worked out all the SmartPoints, making it easy for you to fit them into your eating plan.

LOOK OUT FOR THE SYMBOLS BELOW:

 The number inside the SmartPoints coin tells you how many SmartPoints are in the recipe.

If you're following No Count, you can eat this recipe to your satisfaction without having to count it.

GF A recipe that is totally gluten free, or can be made gluten free with a few simple swaps. Always check labels, as some ingredients, such as baking powder, may contain gluten.

V Indicates a recipe that is vegetarian.

TOP TIPS

for cakes, bakes and puddings

With these simple tips and tricks, you can make sweet treats
that taste great and can fit into your weekly SmartPoints budget.

Watch the toppings
The icing on the cake isn't always a good thing. Instead of butter, use low-fat soft cheese in frosting, and cut back on the icing sugar. Better still, instead of thick buttercreams, try a thin sugar glaze on cakes, or just a light dusting of icing sugar. Try Strawberry & cream cupcakes, p74.

Reduce the sugar
The more sugar we eat, the more we crave, but the good news is our tastebuds can just as quickly get used to less sugar. Cut down on the sweet stuff in recipes and before long you won't even notice it. See page 11 for a rundown of alternatives to refined sugar.

Include fruit & vegetables
Using puréed fruits or grated vegetables in cakes has lots of benefits – it adds natural sweetness and flavour, and will keep cakes moist, so you can use less sugar and fat in the recipe. Carrot, beetroot, courgettes, butternut squash, apples, bananas and berries all work well. Try Chocolate orange swede cake, p60.

Reduce the fat
Many puddings rely on cream or butter to make them taste luxurious but there are lots of other ways to achieve a similar result. Low-fat natural Greek yogurt has a creamy flavour and texture without the saturated fat. Try soya milk in custards or sauces, and low-fat soft cheese in cheesecakes – adding a little gelatin will help chilled puddings set without the fat. Try Raspberry & ginger cheesecake, p68.

Cut down on the carbs
If you want low carb or gluten-free alternatives, make cakes and bakes without using flour. Rolled oats and ground nuts are a popular substitute; you can even make cakes using puréed beans or chickpeas Try Mango, blueberry & lime traybake, p34.

Try alternatives
Use lighter versions of pastry that have less butter in them. Filo is a great alternative to puff or shortcrust – it has all the crispness you want from pastry but much less fat. Try Beautiful plum tarts, p82.

Go big on flavour
Add lots of flavour to recipes and you won't notice there's less sugar and fat. Use cocoa powder instead of chocolate, or add spices such as ginger and cinnamon, and flavours like vanilla, lemon and coffee. Go for fruits that are strong on taste, such as mangos, and apricots, and combine different ingredients. Try Strawberry, rose & pistachio pavlova, p94.

Change the proportions
Love fruit crumbles? You can still enjoy them but use more fruit and less crumble topping. If you're making a fruit pie, have a pastry top, but skip the bottom. And when making cakes, go easy on the added extras, like chocolate chips, dried fruits and nuts – you can still add them, just use less.

Serve smaller portions
A bite-size treat may be all you need to satisfy your desire for something sweet. Make mini muffins or individual desserts in small ramekins, or cut traybakes and cakes into smaller pieces.

What sweetener?

There's no getting away from it – whatever kind of cake or pudding you're making, you'll probably want to add sweetness. But how do you choose what's best? Here's a quick guide:

Sugar

Usually made from sugar cane or beet, processed sugar comes in various forms – including caster, granulated, icing and demerara – and in varying degrees of refinement. As a rule, the darker the colour, the less refined it is and the more nutritional value it has in the form of trace vitamins and minerals. Less refined sugars, such as dark brown sugar, can alter a recipe's flavour and appearance.

Molasses

Also known as black treacle, molasses is a sticky by-product of the sugar refining process. It's about 60% sugar, and contains nutrients such as iron, calcium and other vitamins and minerals. There are different types of molasses; the darker the colour, the less sweet it will be. Molasses has quite a strong flavour, and is often used in dark fruit cakes and gingerbread, but is not

Maple syrup

Made from the sap of the sugar maple tree, maple syrup is about 60% sugar, and has small amounts of nutrients, such as calcium and iron. A classic topping for pancakes, and great for drizzling, it has a distinctive smoky, caramel flavour. Always make sure you read the label and buy a product that says 100% maple syrup – other 'maple-flavoured' syrups are made from processed sugar.

Artificial sweeteners

There's a wide variety of low-calorie or no-calorie artificial sweeteners available, such as saccharin, sucralose and aspartame. Some come in powdered or granulated form, but they can be tricky to bake with as they don't have the same bulk as sugar, and some don't stand up to heat very well – so check the label before buying. They can be useful in chilled desserts such as fools and cheesecakes.

Honey

Honey is great for adding natural sweetness and flavour, but it's about 80% sugar, so use it sparingly. It does provide small amounts of some nutrients, such as B vitamins.

Stevia

Produced from a herb that is many times sweeter than sugar, but without the calories, stevia is available in a powdered form that can be used in baking and desserts. Some stevia products have a licorice-like aftertaste which some people don't like.

Agave nectar

Agave nectar, sometimes called agave syrup, is made from the leaves of the agave plant and is about 65% sugar. Light agave syrup has a neutral flavour, so it's good for sweetening drinks and delicately-flavoured puds. Darker versions have more of a caramel flavour.

Snacks

Great idea

If you don't have a piping bag, use a plastic food bag with one corner snipped off.

SNACKS

Baked 'chai' doughnuts with cinnamon glaze

Thought you couldn't have doughnuts? These baked ones are every bit as good as fried ones.

Makes 6

Prep time
15 minutes plus cooling

Cook time
10-12 minutes

Ingredients
Calorie controlled cooking spray
150g plain flour
25g light brown soft sugar
¼ teaspoon baking powder
¼ teaspoon bicarb of soda
1½ teaspoons cinnamon
Seeds from 8 green cardamom pods, crushed
Pinch of grated nutmeg
½ teaspoon ground cloves
100ml skimmed milk
1 egg, beaten
30g low-fat spread, melted
½ teaspoon vanilla extract
1 teaspoon cider vinegar

For the glaze
2½ tablespoons icing sugar
¼ teaspoon cinnamon
Brown food colouring

1 Preheat the oven to 200°C, fan 180°C, gas mark 6. Mist a 6-hole doughnut tin with cooking spray.

2 Put the flour, sugar, baking powder, bicarb of soda and spices in a large bowl. Add a pinch of salt, then stir to combine and make a well in the centre.

3 In a jug, stir together the milk, egg, melted spread, vanilla extract and cider vinegar. Gradually pour into the flour mixture, stirring constantly to prevent lumps. Spoon into a piping bag fitted with a plain nozzle and pipe into the prepared tin, filling each hole two-thirds full. Bake for 10-12 minutes or until risen and golden, then transfer the doughnuts to a wire rack to cool completely.

4 Make the glaze. Stir together the icing sugar with 2 tablespoons of water and the cinnamon until smooth. Put about half the glaze into a separate bowl and stir in the food colouring.

5 Dip the tops of the doughnuts into the white glaze, then return to the wire rack to set for about 10 minutes. Drizzle over the coloured glaze in a zig-zag pattern to decorate.

SmartPoints values per doughnut 6
SmartPoints values per recipe 38

14

SNACKS

Pear & cranberry streusel bars

Autumnal fruit, oats and crunchy almonds combine in these quick and easy crumble-style bars.

Makes 12

Prep time
10 minutes, plus cooling

Cook time
10-15 minutes

Ingredients
Calorie controlled
cooking spray
50g low-fat spread
75g clear honey
200g rolled oats
50g ground almonds
½ teaspoon almond extract
2 ripe pears, peeled, cored
and chopped
100g fresh (or defrosted
frozen) cranberries

For the streusel
25g low-fat spread
25g plain flour
15g flaked almonds,
roughly chopped
1 tablespoon
demerara sugar

1 Preheat the oven to 220°C, fan 200°C, gas mark 7. Mist a 15cm x 23cm baking tin with cooking spray and line the base with baking paper.

2 Put the low-fat spread and honey in a large pan and gently heat until the spread has melted. Add the remaining main ingredients and stir until well combined. Spoon into the prepared tin and press down firmly with the back of a spoon.

3 To make the streusel topping, use your fingers to rub the low-fat spread and flour together. Stir in the remaining ingredients. Scatter over the oat mixture and press in lightly. Bake for 10-15 minutes, or until firm and golden. Allow to cool in the tin, then turn out onto a board and cut into 12 slices.

SmartPoints values per bar 5
SmartPoints values per recipe 64

Flourless pancakes

Makes 4

Prep time
5 minutes
Cook time
16 minutes

Who'd have thought pancakes could be so easy? Make these in a flash for breakfast or brunch.

Ingredients
4 ripe bananas, mashed
2 large eggs,
lightly beaten
Pinch of salt
Calorie controlled
cooking spray

To serve
4 tablespoons 0% fat
natural Greek yogurt
Fresh berries
4 teaspoons agave syrup

1 In a bowl, mix the banana and egg together, then add the salt.

2 Heat a nonstick frying pan over a medium heat. Mist with cooking spray. Drop a ladleful of the mixture into the pan and swirl. Cook for 2 minutes until golden; flip and cook for another 2 minutes. Repeat so you have 4 pancakes.

3 Serve each pancake topped with some yogurt, berries and 1 teaspoon of agave syrup.

SmartPoints values per pancake 2
SmartPoints values per recipe 9

Marmalade & ginger cookies

Makes 23

Prep time
10 minutes plus cooling

Cook time
15 minutes

These are similar to flapjacks and just the thing if you are looking for a little bit of sweetness.

Ingredients
50g plain flour
¼ teaspoon bicarbonate of soda
1 teaspoon ground ginger
150g rolled oats
50g low-fat spread
75g light brown soft sugar
Grated zest of 1 orange
1 egg, lightly beaten
50g marmalade

1 Preheat the oven to 180°C, fan 160°C, gas mark 4 and line two baking sheets with baking paper.

2 Mix together the flour, bicarbonate of soda and ginger in a bowl, then stir in the oats.

3 In a separate bowl, beat the spread and sugar together until pale and creamy, using a wooden spoon. Using a hand-held electric whisk, beat in the orange zest, egg and marmalade until smooth. Stir in the flour mixture and mix well.

4 Put tablespoonfuls of the mixture on the baking sheets, spaced 2.5cm apart, then flatten the tops slightly with the back of the spoon – you should get 23 biscuits from the mixture. Bake the cookies for 12-15 minutes or until slightly crisp and golden. Transfer to a wire rack to cool.

SmartPoints values per cookie 2
SmartPoints values per recipe 56

SNACKS

Chocolate & orange biscotti

These sweet and crunchy biscotti are the perfect accompaniment to your morning coffee.

Makes 22

Prep time
20 minutes plus cooling

Cook time
45 minutes

Ingredients
200g plain flour
1 teaspoon baking powder
90g caster sugar
2 medium eggs
Grated zest of 1 orange
75g blanched almonds, toasted and roughly chopped
50g dark chocolate chips

1 Preheat the oven to 180°C, fan 160°C, gas mark 4. Line 2 baking sheets with baking paper. Sift the flour and baking powder into a bowl. Add the caster sugar.

2 In a jug, whisk the eggs with the orange zest. Make a well in the centre of the dry ingredients and pour in the egg mixture. Mix until you have a soft dough, then fold in the almonds and chocolate chips.

3 Tip the dough onto a lightly floured surface and shape into 2 x 25cm sausages. Transfer to the prepared baking sheets, leaving room for them to spread as they cook. Bake for 25-30 minutes.

4 Remove from the oven and let cool slightly. Turn the temperature down to 160°C, fan 140°C, gas mark 3. Using a serrated knife, cut the biscotti into 22 x 1cm-thick slices. Arrange side by side, cut-side down, on the baking sheets. Bake for 10 minutes, until crisp and just beginning to turn golden, then turn and bake for another 5 minutes. Cool on a wire rack.

SmartPoints values per biscotti 3
SmartPoints values per recipe 74

SNACKS

Apple & cranberry traybake squares

This fruity traybake looks so tempting. It's great with a cuppa or to put in packed lunches.

Makes 16

Prep time
15 minutes plus cooling

Cook time
30 minutes

Ingredients
50g caster sugar
100g low-fat spread
1 egg
250g chunky apple sauce (from a jar)
150g self-raising flour
1 teaspoon baking powder
1 teaspoon ground cinnamon
40g dried cranberries, chopped
2 apples, cored and thinly sliced

1 Preheat the oven to 180°C, fan 160 °C, gas mark 4. Line a 19cm x 23cm baking tin with baking paper.

2 Reserve ½ teaspoon caster sugar for the top of the cake. Using a hand-held electric whisk, beat the rest of the sugar and the spread together in a large mixing bowl until creamy. Add the egg and the apple sauce, and beat again.

3 Sift in the flour, baking powder and cinnamon, and mix well. Stir in the dried cranberries, then spoon the cake mixture into the prepared tin and spread with the spoon until even.

4 Arrange the sliced apples in four rows on top of the cake. Sprinkle with the reserved sugar, then bake for 25-30 minutes until risen. A skewer inserted into the centre of the cake should come out clean.

5 Cool the cake in the tin for 15 minutes, then turn out onto a wire rack to cool completely. Cut into 16 squares to serve and store in an airtight tin for up to a couple of days, or freeze, well wrapped and labelled.

SmartPoints values per square 4
SmartPoints values per recipe 61

Mango meringue eggs

Perfect for a treat or summery pud – make the meringues in advance and fill just before serving.

Serves 12

Prep time
15 minutes plus cooling

Cook time
1 hour

Ingredients
4 egg whites
1 teaspoon vanilla extract
200g caster sugar
1 mango, flesh only

1 Preheat the oven to 150°C, fan 130°C, gas mark 2. Line two baking sheets with baking paper.

2 In a clean bowl, whisk the egg whites with an electric mixer until they form very stiff peaks, then whisk in the vanilla extract and half the caster sugar.

3 Add the remaining sugar a spoonful at a time, whisking in between until the mixture is stiff again.

4 Spoon onto the lined trays to make 12 nests, creating a small dip in the middle of each. Bake in the oven for 1 hour, turning the heat down to 130°C, fan 110°C, gas mark 1 for the final 20 minutes. Remove from the oven and leave to cool on a wire rack.

5 To serve, blitz the mango in a mini food processor and spoon into the nests.

SmartPoints values per filled meringue 4
SmartPoints values per recipe 49

Cook's tip

Save time by buying ready prepared butternut squash – you'll also avoid waste by only buying what you need.

SNACKS

Butternut squash & chocolate brownies

The butternut squash adds a little sweetness and richness to these moist, chewy brownies.

Makes 12

Prep time
10 minutes plus cooling

Cook time
40 minutes

Ingredients

Calorie controlled cooking spray
300g butternut squash flesh, cut into 2cm pieces
100g dark chocolate, roughly chopped
4 eggs
200g golden caster sugar
50g cocoa powder
75g plain flour
2 teaspoons baking powder
Pinch of salt
Icing sugar, for dusting

1 Preheat the oven to 180°C, fan 160°C, gas mark 4. Mist a 20cm x 20cm baking tin with cooking spray and line with baking paper.

2 Put the squash in a heatproof bowl, splash a little water over and cover with cling film. Microwave on high for 10-12 minutes until tender. Drain off any excess water, then stir in the chocolate – the heat from the squash will melt the chocolate. Using a hand blender, whizz the mixture to a rough purée. Set aside to cool.

3 Using an electric hand-held whisk, beat together the eggs and sugar in a large bowl until the mixture is pale and fluffy. Fold through the cocoa powder, flour, baking powder and salt.

4 Fold in the squash mixture, then pour into the prepared tin. Bake for 25-30 minutes until the brownies have set. Remove from the oven and let cool in the tin for at least 1 hour. Cut into 12 squares and dust with icing sugar to serve.

SmartPoints values per brownie 8
SmartPoints values per recipe 96

White chocolate & cranberry cookies

Makes 12

Prep time
10 minutes plus cooling
Cook time
15 minutes

Dried cranberries add a sharp, tangy flavour that works well with the sweetness of the chocolate.

Ingredients
75g low-fat spread
75g light brown soft sugar
1 egg, lightly beaten
50g white chocolate chips
50g dried cranberries
100g self-raising flour
75g rolled oats

1 Preheat the oven to 180°C, fan 160°C, gas mark 4. Line 2 baking sheets with baking paper. Using a hand-held electric whisk, beat together the low-fat spread and sugar in a large mixing bowl until thick and creamy. Gradually beat in the egg. Stir in the chocolate chips and cranberries, then fold in the flour and oats.

2 Put 12 dessert spoonfuls of the mixture onto the prepared baking sheets, leaving plenty of room between them and press each one down with the back of a spoon to flatten it slightly. Bake for 12-15 minutes until lightly golden and just firm to the touch, then cool on a wire rack until firm. Store in an airtight tin for up to 3 days.

SmartPoints values per cookie 6
SmartPoints values per recipe 71

Fruit skewers with hot chocolate drizzle

Serves 4

Prep time
5 minutes
Cook time
5 minutes

Cool fresh fruit and warm chocolate sauce make the perfect combination for a sweet treat.

Ingredients
8 strawberries
2 bananas
2 kiwi fruit
1 large ripe mango

For the chocolate drizzle
50g plain chocolate
1 tablespoon cocoa powder
1 tablespoon cornflour
200ml skimmed milk

1 First, prepare the fruit. Halve the strawberries, if large; peel and chop the bananas; peel and slice the kiwi fruit; then peel, de-stone and slice the mango. Thread the fruit onto 8 bamboo sticks, alternating the pieces.

2 To make the sauce, break the chocolate into pieces and put them in a pan with the cocoa powder, cornflour and milk. Heat gently over a low-medium heat, stirring constantly, until the sauce is smooth and thickened.

3 Serve 2 fruit skewers per person with the hot chocolate drizzle on the side.

SmartPoints values per serving 5
SmartPoints values per recipe 20

Try this

This recipe works well with other fruit combos, too. Try it with fresh pineapple and raspberries instead of mango and blueberries.

SNACKS

Mango, blueberry & lime traybake

A secret ingredient – chickpeas – helps gives these fruity bars their irresistible flavour and texture.

Makes 12

Prep time
15 minutes plus cooling

Cook time
30 minutes

Ingredients
400g tin chickpeas in water, drained
100g cashew butter
75g maple syrup
2 eggs
Grated zest and juice of 1 lime
2 teaspoons vanilla essence
75g rolled oats (ensure gluten free)
25g desiccated coconut
1 teaspoon baking powder
100g blueberries
50g chopped fresh mango

For the lime drizzle
50g icing sugar
1 teaspoon lime juice
Grated zest of 1 lime, to garnish

1 Preheat the oven to 180°C, fan 160°C, gas mark 4. Grease a 20cm x 20cm baking tin and line with baking paper.

2 Whizz the chickpeas in a food processor with the cashew butter, maple syrup, eggs, lime zest and juice, and vanilla essence, until combined. Spoon into a bowl, add the oats, coconut and baking powder, and mix well. Fold through the blueberries and mango, then pour into the tin, smooth the surface and bake for 30 minutes or until risen and golden.

3 Remove from the oven and cool on a wire rack in the tin for 10 minutes. Remove from the tin and cool completely. Mix the icing sugar and lime juice with 1 tablespoon of water. Drizzle over the traybake, then decorate with the lime zest and cut into 12 squares.

SmartPoints values per square 6
SmartPoints values per recipe 71

Coconut ice bars

Makes 12

Prep time
15 minutes

Put these delicious bites into boxes and tie with a colourful ribbon to make a great foodie gift.

Ingredients
100g unsweetened desiccated coconut
3 tablespoons light condensed milk
100g icing sugar
A few drops of pink food colouring

1 Put the coconut, condensed milk and all but 2 tablespoons of the icing sugar into a large bowl and mix together with a spatula until well combined. The mixture should be very stiff.

2 Divide the mixture in half. Colour one half of the mixture with just a few drops of pink food colouring until pale pink.

3 Dust 2 pieces of baking paper with the remaining icing sugar. Put the white coconut mixture onto one piece of paper and roll out into a rectangle approximately 11cm x 10cm. Repeat the process with the pink mixture on the other sheet.

4 Put the white rectangle on top of the pink rectangle and lightly roll with a rolling pin until stuck together, reshaping the sides to keep the rectangle shape.

5 Leave in a cool place for at least 3 hours or overnight to dry out. Cut into 12 small bars and wrap as desired.

SmartPoints values per bar 5
SmartPoints values per recipe 63

Figgy flapjacks

This easy oaty traybake tastes amazing and uses just a handful of ingredients.

Makes 16

Prep time
5 minutes plus cooling
Cook time
30-35 minutes

Ingredients
Calorie controlled
cooking spray
150g low-fat spread
150g rolled oats (ensure
gluten free)
75g light brown soft sugar
25g toasted hazelnuts,
roughly chopped
Grated zest of ½ orange,
plus 1 tablespoon juice
4 small ripe figs,
roughly chopped

1 Preheat the oven to 190°C, fan 170°C, gas mark 5. Mist a 25cm x 17cm baking tin with cooking spray, line the base with baking paper and set aside.

2 Melt the low-fat spread in a medium pan over a low heat, then add the oats, sugar, hazelnuts, orange zest and juice. Stir until everything is well combined.

3 Scatter the figs over the base of the tin and dot the flapjack mixture over them. Spread and press down with the back of a spoon until the top is level.

4 Bake for 30-35 minutes or until golden. Allow to cool in the tin, then cut into 16 pieces.

SmartPoints values per flapjack 4
SmartPoints values per recipe 59

Cook's tip

If you don't have a round cutter, simply pat the dough out into a rectangle then cut into 12 small squares using a knife.

SNACKS

Simple sultana scones

These easy scones can be whipped up in next to no time if you've got friends popping in for tea.

Makes 12

Prep time
10 minutes plus cooling

Cook time
15 minutes

Ingredients
225g self-raising flour
25g low-fat spread
25g caster sugar
40g sultanas
150g virtually fat-free plain yogurt
2 teaspoons skimmed milk

1 Preheat the oven to 200°C, fan 180°C, gas mark 6. Reserve 2 teaspoons of the flour for rolling (use a little to lightly dust a baking sheet), then sift the rest into a mixing bowl. Rub the spread into the flour until the mixture resembles breadcrumbs.

2 Add the sugar, sultanas and yogurt, using a table knife to mix until you have a soft but not sticky dough that leaves the bowl clean. If you need to, add a little cold water to bring the dough together.

3 Dust the work surface with the reserved flour and pat the dough out by hand to a thickness of 2.5 cm. Use a 5cm-diameter cutter to stamp out as many scones as you can, then reroll the trimmings and stamp out more scones – the mixture should make 12.

4 Put the scones on the baking tray, then brush the tops with the milk. Bake for 12-15 minutes until risen and golden brown. Cool slightly on a wire rack before serving.

SmartPoints values per scone 3
SmartPoints values per recipe 41

Cakes

CAKES

Chocolate berry cake

Serves 10

Prep time
25 minutes plus cooling
Cook time
35-40 minutes

Dark chocolate and tangy berries are perfect together and make this cake great for a special celebration.

Ingredients
150g plain flour
1 teaspoon baking powder
1 teaspoon bicarbonate
of soda
40g cocoa powder
110g low-fat spread
125g caster sugar
2 eggs, beaten
450g raspberries and
strawberries
(fresh or frozen)
25g white chocolate,
melted
25g dark chocolate,
melted

1 Line a 23cm loose-bottomed tin with baking paper. Preheat the oven to 180°C, fan 160°C, gas mark 4.

2 Sift together the flour, baking powder, bicarbonate of soda and cocoa powder. Put in a food processor with the low-fat spread, sugar and eggs, then blend until smooth.

3 Spoon the mixture into the prepared tin and bake for 35-40 minutes or until springy in the middle. Leave in the tin to cool for 5 minutes, then turn out onto a wire rack to cool completely.

4 Slice the cake in half horizontally. Roughly crush two-thirds of the berries with a fork, spread them over one half of the cake and stack the other on top. Arrange the remaining berries on top of the cake – slice the larger ones, if you like. Drizzle the melted chocolate over the fruit and leave to set.

SmartPoints values per serving 8
SmartPoints values per recipe 83

CAKES

Serves 8

Almond & rhubarb cake

Tender rhubarb in a moist almond sponge, this cake is the perfect afternoon pick-me-up.

Prep time
20 minutes plus cooling
Cook time
40 minutes

Ingredients
250g fresh rhubarb,
trimmed and
roughly chopped
40g caster sugar
Juice of 1 orange

For the sponge
100g low-fat spread
70g caster sugar
3 eggs, beaten
70g ground almonds
30g plain flour, sifted
30g flaked almonds

1 Preheat the oven to 180°C, fan 160°C, gas mark 4. Line a 20cm springform tin with baking paper.

2 Put the rhubarb, sugar and orange juice in a pan and cook over a low heat for 6-8 minutes until the rhubarb is nearly tender. Set aside to cool slightly.

3 To make the sponge, beat the low-fat spread with the sugar until light and creamy. Gradually add the eggs and beat well. Fold in the ground almonds and flour.

4 Remove the rhubarb from the pan using a slotted spoon. Fold into the cake mixture, and spoon into the prepared tin. Scatter the flaked almonds over the top and bake for 30 minutes until golden and a skewer inserted into the centre of the cake comes out clean.

5 Let cool in the tin. To turn out, invert onto a plate and remove the paper. Turn the cake the correct way up before slicing and serving.

SmartPoints values per serving 8
SmartPoints values per recipe 67

Inside info

The apple helps give this cake its moistness and sweetness – choose a flavoursome eating variety, such as Cox.

CAKES

Carrot cake with cream cheese frosting

This has all the zesty sweetness of a traditional carrot cake, but with only a third of the SmartPoints.

Serves 10

Prep time
20 minutes plus cooling
Cook time
1 hour 10 minutes

Ingredients
200g gluten-free self-raising flour
1½ teaspoons gluten-free baking powder
1 teaspoon cinnamon
Seeds of 3 cardamom pods, ground
Zest of ½ orange, plus extra to decorate, and 1 teaspoon of the juice
75g low-fat spread
80g light brown soft sugar
2 eggs, lightly beaten
175g grated carrot
50g grated eating apple

For the icing
125g low-fat soft cheese
1 tablespoon icing sugar

1 Preheat the oven to 180°C, fan 160°C, gas mark 4, then line a 900g loaf tin with baking paper.

2 Sift the flour and baking powder into a bowl. Add the cinnamon, ground cardamom and zest of half an orange, and stir to combine.

3 In a separate bowl, beat together the spread and sugar, using a hand-held electric whisk, until light and creamy. Gradually add the eggs, beating well after each addition.

4 Add the flour mixture and mix briefly until just combined. Fold in the grated carrot and apple until evenly distributed. Pour into the loaf tin and bake for 1 hour and 10 minutes, until browned on top and a skewer comes out with just a few wet crumbs. Put the loaf tin on a wire rack and leave until completely cool. Remove the cake from the tin.

5 Once the cake is cool, make the icing. Beat together the cream cheese, icing sugar and the orange juice. Spread over the top of the cake and scatter with orange zest.

SmartPoints values per serving 6
SmartPoints values per recipe 60

CAKES

Sticky gingerbread cake squares

Makes 16

Prep time
5 minutes plus cooling

Cook time
30 minutes

This traditional-style ginger cake is sweetened with molasses, which helps give it a rich, deep flavour.

Ingredients

115g low-fat spread, plus extra for greasing
225g plain flour
1 teaspoon bicarbonate of soda
1 tablespoon ground ginger
1 teaspoon ground cinnamon
200ml dark molasses
2 eggs, lightly beaten
75g stem ginger, drained and roughly chopped, plus 2 tablespoons of the syrup

1 Preheat the oven to 180°C, fan 160°C, gas mark 4. Lightly grease a 20cm x 20cm baking tin and line with baking paper.

2 Sift the flour, bicarbonate of soda, ginger and cinnamon together into a bowl.

3 Melt the spread in a pan over a low heat, allow to cool slightly, then stir in the molasses and eggs.

4 Mix the molasses mixture into the dry ingredients, then stir through most of the stem ginger (reserve 1 tablespoon for the decoration). Pour the mixture into the prepared tin and bake for 30 minutes or until a skewer inserted into the centre of the cake comes out clean.

5 In a pan, warm the reserved syrup with 1 teaspoon water. Pierce holes over the top of the warm cake, then brush over the syrup. Decorate with the reserved stem ginger and leave to cool completely, then cut into 16 squares.

SmartPoints values per square 6
SmartPoints values per recipe 91

Cook's tip

To get maximum volume when whisking egg whites, make sure the bowl and whisk are clean and grease-free.

CAKES

Serves 8

Prep time
25 minutes plus cooling
Cook time
12 minutes

Mixed berry & hazelnut sponge roll

A light-as-air sponge roll that's filled with ice cream and served with summer berries.

Ingredients
3 eggs, separated
100g caster sugar
50g blanched hazelnuts, toasted, then whizzed until finely ground
25g gluten-free plain flour
1 teaspoon baking powder
1 tablespoon unsweetened almond milk (or any other milk)
300g reduced-fat ice cream
400g frozen summer fruits, defrosted slightly
½ tablespoon icing sugar, plus extra for dusting
1 tablespoon lemon juice

1 Preheat the oven to 180°C, fan 160°C, gas mark 4. Line a 33cm x 23cm baking tin with baking paper.

2 Using an electric whisk, beat the egg yolks with 80g of the caster sugar for 3-4 minutes, until pale and thickened. Whisk in the hazelnuts, flour and baking powder. Stir in the milk. In a clean bowl, whisk the egg whites until stiff peaks form, then gently fold them into the cake mixture.

3 Pour the mixture into the tin and bake for 10-12 minutes, or until the sponge springs back when touched gently. Remove from the oven and cool in the tin. Let the ice cream soften out of the freezer for 5-10 minutes. Dust a sheet of baking paper with the reserved caster sugar and turn the sponge onto it.

4 Whizz 100g of the fruit with the icing sugar and lemon juice to make a coulis. Add a little water if it is too thick.

5 Peel the lining paper from the sponge and spread the ice cream over, leaving a 2cm border. Scatter 150g of the summer fruits over, then carefully roll the sponge. Serve with the coulis, the remaining berries and a dusting of icing sugar.

SmartPoints values per serving 8
SmartPoints values per recipe 66

CAKES

Crunchy coffee meringue cake

This unique cake looks – and tastes – spectacular! Try making it for a special occasion.

Serves 12

Prep time
15 minutes plus cooling
Cook time
35 minutes

Ingredients
Calorie controlled cooking spray
100g low-fat spread
80g caster sugar
2 eggs
100g self-raising flour,
½ teaspoon baking powder
2 teaspoons coffee granules (made up with 3 tablespoons boiling water)

For the meringue
2 egg whites
80g caster sugar
2 tablespoons artificial sweetener

For the filling
80g light mascarpone
50g icing sugar
4 tsp cocoa powder

1 Preheat the oven to 180°C, fan 160°C, gas mark 4. Mist a 20cm round cake tin with cooking spray. Trace the outline of the tin on baking paper and put on a baking sheet.

2 Make the meringue. In a bowl, whisk the egg whites until stiff. Add half the sugar and half the sweetener and continue to whisk until the mixture forms stiff peaks. Repeat with the remaining sugar and sweetener. Gently fold in 1 teaspoon of the coffee liquid. Spoon the meringue onto the baking paper, within the traced circle. Set aside while you make the cake.

3 In a bowl, beat together the spread and sugar until pale and fluffy, then gradually beat in the eggs until well combined. Gently fold in the flour, baking powder and remaining coffee, then pour into the prepared tin.

4 Bake the cake and the meringue for 20 minutes. Remove the cake from the oven and turn onto a wire rack to cool. Cook the meringue for a further 10-15 minutes. Set aside to cool.

5 For the filling, beat together all the ingredients until smooth. Spoon the filling over the sponge and top with the meringue.

SmartPoints values per serving 8
SmartPoints values per recipe 99

CAKES

Fresh berry sponge

What a classic! A lovely light sponge topped with fresh fruit – perfect for a summer afternoon tea.

Serves 8

Prep time
25 minutes plus cooling

Cook time
9 minutes

Ingredients
Calorie controlled cooking spray
3 large eggs
100g caster sugar
100g plain flour
200g low-fat soft cheese
Grated zest of 1 lemon
1 tablespoon icing sugar
2 tablespoons lemon curd, mixed with 1 tablespoon hot water
200g raspberries
100g blueberries
Fresh mint leaves, to decorate

1 Preheat the oven to 220°C, fan 200°C, gas mark 7. Mist two 18cm sandwich tins with the cooking spray and line the bases with circles of baking paper.

2 Using a hand-held electric whisk, beat the eggs and sugar in a large bowl until very pale and light in texture – this will take about 5 minutes on full power. Sift the flour into the mixture and fold it through using a large metal spoon. Divide the mixture between the prepared tins and level the tops.

3 Bake for 8-9 minutes until golden brown and springy to the touch. Remove from the oven and turn out of the tins onto a cooling rack. Cover with a clean damp tea towel and leave until completely cold. Remove the lining paper.

4 Mix together the soft cheese, lemon zest and icing sugar. Spread half the mixture over the top of one sponge, then spread the lemon curd over it. Top with most of the raspberries and blueberries. Sandwich the two cakes together and decorate the top with the rest of the soft cheese mixture, the remaining berries and the mint leaves.

SmartPoints values per serving 7
SmartPoints values per recipe 55

CAKES

Apple & maple syrup cupcakes

Topped with a cream cheese frosting and an apple crisp, these cupcakes are deliciously different.

Makes 12

Prep time
20 minutes

Cook time
1 hour
20 minutes

Ingredients
2 apples, peeled, cored
and finely chopped
125g low-fat spread
130g maple syrup
1 teaspoon vanilla
bean paste
2 eggs
200g plain flour
1 teaspoon baking powder
1 teaspoon mixed spice

For the decoration
2 red apples, very thinly
sliced, pips removed
Cinnamon, for dusting

For the frosting
100g low-fat soft cheese
30g low-fat spread
1½ tablespoons maple syrup
⅛ teaspoon mixed spice

1 Put the chopped apples in a pan with a splash of cold water. Cover and simmer over a moderate heat for 8-10 minutes until soft. Remove from the heat, roughly mash and let cool.

2 Preheat oven to 190°C, fan 170°C, gas mark 5. Line a 12-hole muffin tin with paper cases. Put the spread, maple syrup and vanilla in a freestanding mixer, and beat well until combined. Add the eggs, one at a time, beating as you add them.

3 Fold in the flour, baking powder and mixed spice until you have a smooth batter, then fold through the mashed apple. Divide the mixture between the paper cases and bake for 20 minutes, or until risen and golden. Leave to cool completely.

4 Reduce the oven to 120°C, fan 100°C, gas mark ½. For the decoration, line a tray with baking paper and arrange the apple slices on it in a single layer. Dust with cinnamon and bake for 45 minutes to 1 hour until crisp. Set aside to cool.

5 Make the frosting. Whisk all the ingredients together in a bowl until combined, then chill for 1 hour in the fridge. Spread over the cupcakes and top with a dried apple slice.

SmartPoints values per cupcake 6
SmartPoints values per recipe 77

Chocolate orange swede cake

Serves 12

Prep time
15 minutes plus cooling

Cook time
50 minutes

Grated swede adds richness and depth to this flavour-packed cake, without any extra SmartPoints.

Ingredients
Calorie controlled
cooking spray
225g plain flour
1 teaspoon baking powder
1 teaspoon bicarbonate
of soda
3 tablespoons cocoa powder
150g caster sugar
225g grated swede
Juice of 1 orange
2 eggs, lightly beaten
1 teaspoon vanilla extract
100g low-fat spread, melted

To decorate
100g low-fat soft cheese
2 tablespoons icing sugar
150g fresh blackberries

1 Preheat the oven to 180°C, fan 160°C, gas mark 4. Mist a 20cm round cake tin with cooking spray.

2 Sift the flour, baking powder, bicarbonate of soda and cocoa powder into a large bowl. Stir in the sugar, swede, orange juice, eggs and vanilla extract until combined. Stir in the melted spread.

3 Pour the batter into the prepared tin and bake for 50 minutes, or until a skewer inserted into the centre of the cake comes out clean. Cool in the tin for 15 minutes then turn out onto a wire rack to cool completely.

4 Beat together the soft cheese and icing sugar until smooth. Spread over the cake and decorate with the blackberries.

SmartPoints values per serving 7
SmartPoints values per recipe 85

Angel food cupcakes

These little sponge cakes are light and airy – pile on the fresh fruit to make them look really tempting.

Makes 12

Prep time
20 minutes plus cooling

Cook time
15 minutes

Ingredients
5 egg whites
½ teaspoon cream of tartar
Pinch of salt
135g icing sugar, sifted
½ teaspoon vanilla bean paste
45g plain flour, sifted
10g cornflour, sifted

To decorate
100g 0% fat natural Greek yogurt
1 tablespoon stem ginger syrup
Fresh fruit (try nectarines, blackberries, blueberries, redcurrants and pomegranate seeds)

1 Preheat the oven to 180°C, fan 160°C, gas mark 4. Line a 12-hole muffin tin with paper cases.

2 Put the egg whites in the bowl of a freestanding mixer and add the cream of tartar and pinch of salt. Whisk with the balloon whisk attachment until white and fluffy, and then start adding the sugar, a couple of tablespoonfuls at a time, whisking well between each addition.

3 Use a metal spoon to gently fold the vanilla bean paste and half of the plain flour into the egg white mixture until well incorporated, taking care not to knock out any of the air. Fold in the remaining plain flour and the cornflour.

4 Divide the cake mixture between the paper cases and bake for 15 minutes, or until golden and a skewer inserted into the middle of one of the cakes comes out clean.

5 Remove from the oven and allow to cool. Whisk together the yogurt and stem ginger syrup until smooth and combined. Spread the yogurt icing over the top of the cupcakes and decorate with the fresh fruit.

SmartPoints values per cupcake 4
SmartPoints values per recipe 43

Cook's tip

Spooning the syrup over the cake while it is still warm will help it soak in and flavour the cake.

CAKES

Serves 10

Prep time
20 minutes plus cooling

Cook time
50 minutes

Honey, orange & almond cake

This delicious gluten-free cake is made with ground almonds and drizzled with a sticky, tangy syrup.

Ingredients
½ teaspoon low-fat spread, for greasing
6 eggs, separated
100g caster sugar
Grated zest of 3 oranges and juice of ½ orange
150g ground almonds

For the topping
Juice of 1½ oranges
2 tablespoons clear honey
1 orange, peeled and cut into thin rounds

1 Preheat the oven to 180°C, fan 160°C, gas mark 4. Grease the sides of a 20cm springform cake tin and line the base with baking paper. Using a hand-held electric whisk, beat together the egg yolks, caster sugar, orange zest, the juice of half of an orange and the ground almonds in a large bowl.

2 In a separate bowl, whisk the egg whites using a clean whisk for about 2 minutes until they form stiff peaks. Using a metal spoon, fold a spoonful into the cake mixture to loosen it, then fold in the remaining egg whites. Pour the mixture into the prepared tin and bake for 35-40 minutes or until a skewer inserted into the centre of the cake comes out clean. Leave to cool in the tin for about 20 minutes.

3 To make the topping, put the orange juice and honey in a small pan and bring to the boil. Stir once, then cook without stirring for 6-8 minutes until reduced and syrupy.

4 Remove the cake from the tin and, using a fork, prick the top all over, then spoon over three-quarters of the syrup. Arrange the orange slices on top of the cake and spoon over the remaining syrup.

SmartPoints values per serving 7
SmartPoints values per recipe 73

CAKES

Marbled chocolate & banana loaf

This is a lovely, moist banana cake that gives you a hit of chocolate at the same time.

Serves 12

Prep time
20 minutes
Cook time
50-60 minutes

Ingredients
25g cocoa powder, sifted
450g ripe bananas
(unpeeled weight),
peeled and mashed
2 eggs, beaten
½ teaspoon vanilla extract
225g self-raising flour
110g low-fat spread
110g light-brown
soft sugar

1 Line a 900g loaf tin with baking paper. Dissolve the cocoa powder in 4 tablespoons of boiling water and set aside to cool. Preheat the oven to 180°C, fan 160°C, gas mark 4.

2 In a small bowl, mix the bananas, eggs and vanilla. Sift the flour into a separate bowl and rub in the spread with your fingers. Stir in the sugar and the banana mixture. Put a third of the mixture in the small bowl and stir in the cocoa mixture.

3 Put random dollops of each cake mixture in the tin until you've used all the mixture, then swirl with a knife to create a marbled effect.

4 Bake for 50-60 minutes or until golden and a skewer inserted into the centre of the cake comes out clean. Leave for 10 minutes, then turn out onto a wire rack to cool.

SmartPoints values per serving 6
SmartPoints values per recipe 70

Inside info

Stevia is a naturally sourced sweetener that's 250-300 times sweeter than sugar, but without the calories.

CAKES

Raspberry & ginger cheesecake

This classic set cheesecake is sweetened with stevia and topped with fresh berries.

Serves 8

Prep time
15 minutes
plus chilling

Cook time
5 minutes

Ingredients
75g low-fat spread
175g stem ginger
oat biscuits
2 sheets of platinum-
grade leaf gelatine
250g low-fat soft cheese,
at room temperature
200g reduced-fat
crème fraîche
Grated zest of ½ lemon,
plus 2 tablespoons juice
2 sachets powdered
stevia extract
150g fresh raspberries

1 Melt the spread in a small pan over a low heat. Use a little to grease an 18cm springform cake tin. Put the biscuits in a large food bag, seal, then crush into fine crumbs with a rolling pin. Combine with the remaining spread, then press firmly into the base of the prepared tin, using the back of a spoon to ensure it's level. Chill in the fridge for 1 hour.

2 Soak the gelatine in cold water for 5 minutes until softened. Drain, then squeeze out any excess water.

3 Meanwhile, combine the soft cheese and crème fraîche in a bowl. Stir in the lemon zest, juice and stevia, then set aside.

4 Melt the softened gelatine, stirring, in a small pan over a low heat – this should take about 1-2 minutes. Remove from the heat and whisk in a large spoonful of the soft-cheese mixture until combined. Pour the contents of the pan into the remaining soft-cheese mixture and stir until combined.

5 Spoon the filling onto the biscuit base and smooth the top. Chill for a minimum of 3 hours or until firm. Carefully release from the tin and decorate with the raspberries.

SmartPoints values per serving 7
SmartPoints values per recipe 59

CAKES

Chocolate muffins

Who doesn't love a chocolate muffin? These use chocolate and cocoa powder for double the flavour.

Makes 12

Prep time
10 minutes plus cooling

Cook time
15 minutes

Ingredients
150g plain flour
15g cocoa powder
1 teaspoon baking powder
½ teaspoon bicarbonate of soda
60g caster sugar
2 tablespoons honey
1 teaspoon vanilla extract
1 tablespoon vegetable oil
100ml buttermilk
2 eggs, beaten
40g dark chocolate chips

1 Preheat the oven to 180°C, fan 160°C, gas mark 4 and line a 12-hole muffin tin with paper cases.

2 Sift the flour, cocoa powder, baking powder and bicarbonate of soda together in a large mixing bowl, then mix in the caster sugar.

3 In a separate bowl, beat the honey, vanilla extract, oil, buttermilk and eggs together. Add to the flour mixture and stir until just combined. Fold the chocolate chips through.

4 Divide the mixture between the paper cases and bake for 15 minutes, then remove from the oven and leave to cool on a wire rack.

SmartPoints values per muffin 6
SmartPoints values per recipe 68

CAKES

Dorset pear cake

Serves 12

Prep time
15 minutes plus cooling
Cook time
50 minutes

A lovely traditional-style cake that's kept
really fresh by adding pears to the mixture.

Ingredients
100g low-fat spread, plus
½ teaspoon for greasing
2 just-ripe pears, peeled,
cored and cut into
bite-size pieces
A squeeze of lemon juice
1 teaspoon ground
cinnamon
100g caster sugar,
plus 1 teaspoon to serve
225g self-raising flour
1 large egg, lightly beaten
6-7 tablespoons
skimmed milk

1 Preheat the oven to 180°C, fan 160°C, gas mark 4. Grease
the sides of a 20cm x 20cm baking tin and line the base
with baking paper.

2 Put the pears in a bowl and toss them in the lemon juice
to prevent them from discolouring. Add the cinnamon and
1 teaspoon of the sugar, and mix until combined. Set aside.

3 Put the flour in a mixing bowl and rub in the spread with your
fingertips until the mixture resembles breadcrumbs. Mix in
the remaining sugar (reserving 1 teaspoonful to serve), and
the egg and milk to make a soft dough – you may not need
all the milk. Put half of the dough into the cake tin and gently
press it out into an even layer.

4 Scatter the pears evenly over the top. Put the rest of the
dough on top of the pears, spreading it evenly to cover them
completely. Bake for 40-50 minutes until risen and golden.
Leave to cool in the tin for 5 minutes, then turn out onto a
wire rack. Put a plate over the cake and flip it over again,
then sprinkle over the reserved sugar and leave to cool.
Cut into 12 squares.

SmartPoints values per serving 5
SmartPoints values per recipe 64

Strawberry & cream cupcakes

Makes 12

Prep time
15 minutes plus cooling

Cook time
15 minutes

Make these easy cupcakes ahead of time and put the topping on just before you want to serve them.

Ingredients
100g self-raising flour
½ teaspoon baking powder
100g caster sugar
100g low-fat spread
2 eggs, lightly beaten
1 teaspoon vanilla extract
2 tablespoons skimmed milk

For the cream cheese icing
75g low-fat soft cheese
1 teaspoon vanilla extract
2 teaspoons icing sugar
6 strawberries, halved

1 Preheat the oven to 180°C, fan 160°C, gas mark 4 and line a 12-hole muffin tin with paper cases.

2 Sift the flour and baking powder into a large mixing bowl, then stir in the sugar. Add the low-fat spread, eggs, vanilla extract and milk. Using a hand-held electric whisk or wooden spoon, beat everything together for 3 minutes or until light and fluffy.

3 Spoon the mixture into the paper cases and bake for 12-15 minutes until risen and golden. Leave to cool in the tin for a few minutes, then remove and cool on a wire rack.

4 To make the icing, mix together the soft cheese, vanilla extract and icing sugar until smooth and creamy. Spread some of the icing over the top of each cake and finish with half a strawberry.

SmartPoints values per cupcake 5
SmartPoints values per recipe 56

Puddings

PUDDINGS

Quickie fruit crumble

Serve this simple fruit crumble for pudding, or you could even try it for breakfast.

Serves 4

Prep time
15 minutes

Cook time
15 minutes

Ingredients
8 plums
100ml unsweetened apple juice
1 large orange
Pinch of ground cinnamon or mixed spice
25g low-fat spread
75g low-sugar muesli
2 teaspoons demerara sugar

1 Pit and slice the plums. Put them in a pan with the apple juice, a strip of orange zest (use a potato peeler) and the cinnamon or mixed spice. Simmer gently over a low-medium heat for 8-10 minutes, until tender.

2 Meanwhile, finely grate 1 teaspoon of zest from the orange and set aside. Peel the orange with a sharp, serrated knife, removing all the pith, then cut the flesh into segments and set them aside. Put the grated zest into another small pan with the low-fat spread and heat gently until melted. Remove from the heat, stir in the muesli and set aside.

3 Remove the strip of zest from the pan containing the plums. Stir the orange segments into the plum mixture, then divide the fruit between 4 ramekins or heatproof dishes.

4 Preheat the grill. Spoon the muesli mixture on top of the fruit and sprinkle each portion with ½ teaspoon demerara sugar. Grill for 2-3 minutes.

SmartPoints values per serving 4
SmartPoints values per recipe 17

PUDDINGS

Hedgerow jellies

Serves 4

Prep time
10 minutes, plus
cooling and chilling

Ingredients
4 sheets leaf gelatine
500ml clear apple juice
Juice of ½ lemon
1 cinnamon stick
50g caster sugar
150g blackberries

A simple summertime pud – you can mix and match the fruit and flavours to your taste.

1 Put the sheets of gelatine in a bowl, pour in cold water to cover, and leave to soak for 5 minutes until soft.

2 Meanwhile, put the apple juice, lemon juice, cinnamon stick and sugar in a saucepan. Heat gently, stirring until the sugar dissolves, then simmer for 2 minutes. Remove from the heat.

3 Lift the softened gelatine out of the water and squeeze to remove the excess water. Add to the hot spiced apple juice and stir. The gelatine will dissolve almost immediately. Leave the liquid to cool, then remove the cinnamon stick.

4 Divide the blackberries between 4 glasses or ramekins, then pour the jelly mixture on top.

5 Cover with cling film and chill in the fridge for 2 hours or until firm.

SmartPoints values per serving 6
SmartPoints values per recipe 23

Cook's tip...

Keep filo pastry covered with a damp cloth until you need it, to prevent it from drying out.

PUDDINGS

Beautiful plum tarts

Light, crisp filo pastry is topped with frangipane and slices of juicy plums in this heavenly dessert.

Makes 8

Prep time
20 minutes
Cook time
25 minutes

Ingredients
Calorie controlled
cooking spray
6 x 45g sheets of filo
pastry, thawed if frozen
1 egg, beaten
50g ground almonds
25g caster sugar
4 plums, halved, pitted
and sliced thinly
1 teaspoon icing sugar,
to decorate

1 Preheat the oven to 180°C, fan 160°C, gas mark 4. Lightly spray 2 baking sheets with the cooking spray.

2 Unroll the filo pastry sheets, and cut them into 8 equal squares. Layer the squares on the baking sheet in 8 piles, misting each layer of pastry with a little of cooking spray, and offsetting the squares as you layer them to make a rough circle.

3 Reserve 1 tablespoon of beaten egg, then mix the rest with the ground almonds and sugar. Divide this mixture between the pastry circles, spreading it in the middle to leave a border round the edge. Top the almond mixture with the sliced plums. Brush the pastry borders with the reserved egg and scrunch up the pastry a little around the filling.

4 Bake for 20-25 minutes, until the pastry is golden brown. Serve the tarts warm, sprinkled with a little icing sugar.

SmartPoints values per serving 5
SmartPoints values per recipe 40

PUDDINGS

Serves 4

Prep time
15 minutes, plus chilling

Ingredients
450g strawberries, hulled
2 large egg whites
2 tablespoons
caster sugar
2 teaspoons
vanilla extract
125ml thick low-fat
natural yogurt

Strawberry posset

Fresh strawberries and zingy yogurt combine in this dreamy dessert that takes minutes to make.

1 Reserve 8 strawberries and purée the rest in a blender – or put them in a large bowl and purée with a hand-held blender.

2 Whisk the egg whites in a clean, grease-free bowl for about 1 minute until they form soft peaks. Gradually whisk in the caster sugar until the mixture forms stiff, glossy peaks.

3 Mix together the vanilla extract and yogurt, then gradually fold in the egg whites using a metal spoon – try to keep as much air in the mixture as possible.

4 Fold in the strawberry purée to make lovely swirls of the fruit. Spoon the mixture into 4 glasses and chill for 30 minutes. Top with the reserved strawberries to serve.

SmartPoints values per serving 3
SmartPoints values per recipe 10

Cook's tip
If you're having trouble turning out the set puds, dip the pudding basins into warm water for a few seconds first.

PUDDINGS

White chocolate puds with raspberry sauce

These cool, creamy set puds are served with a vibrant raspberry sauce and fresh berries.

Serves 4

Prep time
15 minutes plus chilling

Cook time
5 minutes

Ingredients
Calorie controlled cooking spray
4 sheets leaf gelatine
300ml skimmed milk
25g caster sugar
40g white chocolate, roughly chopped
150g fat-free natural yogurt
4 tablespoons reduced-fat crème fraîche
½ teaspoon vanilla extract
250g raspberries
1 tablespoon icing sugar

1 Spray 4 mini pudding basins or ramekins with cooking spray. Submerge the gelatine in a bowl of cold water and leave to soak for about 5 minutes.

2 Heat the milk and sugar in a pan until starting to bubble at the edges. Remove the pan from the heat.

3 Squeeze the excess water from the gelatine and add to the hot milk, stir to dissolve, then stir in the white chocolate until it has melted. Cool the mixture to room temperature.

4 In a mixing bowl, whisk together the yogurt, crème fraîche and vanilla extract, then blend in the white chocolate milk. Pour into the prepared pudding basins, cover with cling film and chill in the fridge for 2 hours or until set.

5 Make the sauce by blending 150g of the raspberries with the icing sugar. Sieve the sauce to remove the seeds.

6 Turn the puds out of their basins. Top with the remaining raspberries and drizzle with the raspberry sauce.

SmartPoints values per serving 8
SmartPoints values per recipe 31

PUDDINGS

Baked custard tart

Who could resist a traditional custard tart? This easy version is made with light ready-made pastry.

Serves 8

Prep time
10 minutes plus chilling
Cook time
40 minutes

Ingredients
150g light shortcrust
pastry sheet
2 eggs
25g caster sugar
300ml skimmed milk
A good pinch of
grated nutmeg

1 Preheat the oven to 200°C, fan 180°C, gas mark 6. Roll the pastry out quite thinly and use it to line an 18cm fluted tart case. Line the pastry case with baking paper and fill it with baking beans. Bake for 10 minutes, remove the paper and beans and then bake for a further 5 minutes or until the pastry is a light golden colour.

2 Reduce the oven temperature to 180°C, fan 160°C, gas mark 4. Beat the eggs and caster sugar together in a large bowl. Warm the milk gently and pour it over the egg mixture. Beat well and then strain through a fine sieve into a jug. Carefully pour the custard into the pastry case, sprinkle with the nutmeg and bake for 25 minutes or until just set. Allow to cool, remove from the tin and chill before serving.

SmartPoints values per serving 5
SmartPoints values per recipe 38

PUDDINGS

Serves 2

Prep time
5 minutes
Cook time
35 minutes

Poached apricots with maple pecans

A luxurious pud of fresh apricots poached with maple syrup and served with crunchy pecan nuts.

Ingredients
1 tablespoon maple syrup
1 tablespoon caster sugar
1 vanilla pod, split in
half horizontally
6 apricots, halved
and de-stoned
25g unsalted pecans,
chopped
150g 0% fat natural
Greek yogurt

1 Put 300ml water in a small pan (just large enough to fit all the apricots in one layer) and add the maple syrup, caster sugar and halved vanilla pod. Bring to the boil over a very low heat, allowing the sugar to dissolve, then add the apricots and simmer for 4-5 minutes, or until the fruit is soft.

2 Lift the apricots out with a slotted spoon and drain on kitchen paper. Turn up the heat and simmer the liquid for 12-15 minutes, or until reduced and starting to form large bubbles. Stir in the nuts and cook for 1-2 minutes until coated.

3 Serve the apricots with the Greek yogurt, topped with the syrupy pecans.

SmartPoints values per serving 8
SmartPoints values per recipe 15

PUDDINGS

Watermelon granita

Serves 4

Prep time
10 minutes plus freezing
Cook time
2 minutes

Nothing says summer like watermelon, especially when it's turned into this refreshing iced dessert.

Ingredients
900g watermelon
100ml cranberry juice
20g sugar
Grated zest and juice of
1 small lemon

1 Cut the watermelon into chunks, reserving four small slices to decorate, then remove the flesh and seeds from the skin. Mash with the back of a fork to a rough purée – it should contain small chunks as well as a few of the seeds.

2 Put the cranberry juice and sugar in a small pan and bring to the boil for 1–2 minutes until the sugar dissolves. Remove from the heat.

3 Mix the lemon zest and juice into the watermelon, along with the cranberry syrup. Spoon into a lidded freezer-proof container and freeze for 1 hour. Remove from the freezer and scrape the ice crystals around the edge into the middle using a fork. Return to the freezer and repeat the freezing and stirring twice more. Serve in chilled glasses decorated with the watermelon slices.

SmartPoints values per serving 2
SmartPoints values per recipe 8

PUDDINGS

Strawberry rose & pistachio pavlova

This beautiful dessert is really simple to make – and great served for a special occasion.

Serves 6

Prep time
20 minutes

Cook time
1 hour 30 minutes

Ingredients
3 egg whites
¼ teaspoon cream of tartar
175g caster sugar
15g pistachios, finely chopped
1 tablespoon rosewater
300g 0% fat natural Greek yogurt
225g strawberries, hulled and quartered

1 Preheat the oven to 150°C, fan 130°C, gas mark 2. In a very clean, grease-free bowl, whisk the egg whites and cream of tartar until stiff peaks form. Continue to whisk, gradually adding the sugar one spoonful at a time to make a really thick, glossy meringue.

2 Line a baking tray with baking paper and tip the meringue onto the tray in a rectangle about 22cm x 17cm. Using the back of a wet spoon, level the top of the pavlova, leaving it slightly higher at the edges to make a rim. Scatter the pistachios over and put into the oven. Immediately reduce the oven temperature to 140°C, fan 120°C, gas mark 1 and cook for 1 hour 30 minutes or until dry on the outside. Turn off the oven and leave to go cold.

3 To serve, remove the meringue from the baking paper and put on a serving plate. Mix the rosewater into the Greek yogurt and spread over the middle of the meringue. Top with the strawberries and serve immediately.

SmartPoints values per serving 8
SmartPoints values per recipe 50

PUDDINGS

Apricot & raspberry popovers

Serves 6

Prep time
10 minutes

Cook time
25 minutes

A bit like sweet Yorkshire puds, these are studded
with pieces of fruit and served with warm custard.

Ingredients

411g tin apricot halves
in juice, drained
75g plain flour
Pinch of salt
25g caster sugar
2 eggs
½ teaspoon vanilla extract
175ml skimmed milk
Calorie controlled
cooking spray
150g raspberries
500g carton low-fat
custard, to serve
½ teaspoon icing sugar,
to dust

1 Preheat the oven to 200°C, fan 180°C, gas mark 6. Put
a 12-hole non-stick muffin tin in the oven to preheat.

2 Cut the apricot halves in two and pat dry on absorbent
kitchen paper.

3 Sift the flour into a mixing bowl with the salt, then stir in the
caster sugar. Make a well in the centre and break in the eggs.
Add the vanilla extract and gradually whisk together, adding
the milk as you go.

4 Spray the hot muffin tin with the cooking spray. Pour in the
batter to make 12 popovers. Drop the apricot pieces and
whole raspberries into the batter, then bake on the centre
shelf for 20-25 minutes until the popovers are puffed up,
golden brown and set.

5 Meanwhile, heat the custard. Remove the hot popovers from
the tin and dust with icing sugar. Serve 2 of the popovers
per person, with the warm custard poured over the top.

SmartPoints values per serving 6
SmartPoints values per recipe 36

PUDDINGS

Rhubarb & apple crisp

Serves 6

Prep time
15 minutes
Cook time
40 minutes

This easy dessert is full of fruity flavour – it's the perfect choice for a family weekend meal.

Ingredients
350g rhubarb, trimmed and cut into 1.5cm pieces
2 eating apples, peeled, cored and cut into 1cm chunks
2 teaspoons cornflour
50g stem ginger, drained and roughly chopped
50g low-fat spread, cut into small cubes
75g rolled oats (ensure gluten free)
20g light brown soft sugar
½ teaspoon ground cinnamon

1 Preheat the oven to 190°C, fan 170°C, gas mark 5. Put the rhubarb and apples in an ovenproof dish (about 20cm long and 4cm deep) and sprinkle over the cornflour. Toss to coat all the pieces. Stir in the stem ginger, add a splash of cold water and cook, uncovered, in the oven for 15 minutes.

2 Meanwhile, rub the low-fat spread into the oats, then stir in the sugar and cinnamon.

3 Sprinkle the oat mixture all over the fruit and return to the oven for another 25 minutes, until golden. Serve warm.

SmartPoints values per serving 5
SmartPoints values per recipe 30

Cook's tip

Keep your eye on the meringue when the puddings are under the grill as it can easily burn.

PUDDINGS

Cherry meringue pies

A twist on a popular classic, the meringue topping simply needs flashing under a hot grill.

Serves 4

Prep time
15 minutes plus chilling
Cook time
7 minutes

Ingredients
75g light digestive biscuits
25g low-fat spread
350g frozen stoned dark cherries, defrosted
1 teaspoon caster sugar
1 slightly heaped teaspoon cornflour

For the meringue
1 large egg white
1 tablespoon caster sugar

1 Crush the biscuits in a blender or put them in a plastic bag and crush with a rolling pin until you have fine crumbs. Put the crumbs in a bowl. Melt the spread and mix it into the crumbs. Divide between 4 large (150 ml) ramekins and press with the back of a spoon to form firm bases. Set aside.

2 Put the cherries and sugar in a pan. Put a little of the juice from the cherries into a cup and stir in the cornflour. Heat the cherries and, when warm, stir in the cornflour mixture and cook for 2 minutes over a medium-low heat until thickened. Using a hand-blender, partially blend the cherries to a coarse purée. Spoon onto the biscuit bases and chill for 15 minutes.

3 Preheat the grill to medium-high. Put the egg whites in a clean, grease-free bowl and whisk until it forms stiff peaks. Add the sugar and whisk to a firm, glossy meringue. Spoon a quarter of the meringue on top of each ramekin.

4 Put the ramekins on a baking tray and put under the grill for 1 minute until they start to turn golden. Remove from the heat and leave to cool for a couple of minutes before serving.

SmartPoints values per serving 5
SmartPoints values per recipe 21

Inside info

Clafoutis is a French pudding traditionally made with cherries. It's best served still warm from the oven.

PUDDINGS

Serves 6

Prep time
10 minutes

Cook time
45 minutes

Apricot & pistachio clafoutis

Tender fruit is covered in a custard-like batter and topped with crunchy pistachio nuts.

Ingredients
Calorie-controlled cooking spray
2 eggs
75g caster sugar
1 teaspoon vanilla extract
100g self-raising flour
100g low-fat natural yogurt
100ml semi-skimmed milk
¼ teaspoon almond extract
2 x 411g tins apricots in juice
20g pistachios, roughly chopped
1 teaspoon icing sugar

1 Preheat the oven to 180°C, fan 160°C, gas mark 4 and mist a 1-litre shallow ovenproof dish with the cooking spray.

2 Whisk the eggs together with the caster sugar and vanilla extract for about 4-5 minutes, or until light and fluffy, then add the flour and whisk again until smooth. Stir in the yogurt, milk and almond extract.

3 Drain the apricots and put them into the greased dish, then pour the mixture on top. Scatter the pistachios over and bake for 45 minutes until golden. Dust with icing sugar, then serve straight away.

SmartPoints values per serving 7
SmartPoints values per recipe 42

Raspberry zabaglione

This is a simple dessert that's great for entertaining. Serve in pretty glass dishes for maximum effect.

Serves 4

Prep time
5 minutes, plus cooling

Cook time
5 minutes

Ingredients
250g raspberries
Juice of ½ lemon
2 teaspoons icing sugar
4 egg yolks
1 tablespoon caster sugar
4 tablespoons Prosecco

1 Put 175g raspberries and the lemon juice into a food processor and blitz to a purée, then pass through a sieve to remove the seeds. Stir in the icing sugar and set aside.

2 Put the egg yolks, caster sugar and Prosecco into a heatproof bowl over a pan of gently simmering water. Use a hand-held electric whisk to whisk the mixture for 5 minutes, until it is thickened and light and holds its shape. Remove from the heat and continue to whisk until the mixture has fully cooled.

3 Carefully fold in the raspberry purée. Put the remaining raspberries into four bowls (reserving a few for the top), then spoon the zabaglione on top. Decorate with the reserved raspberries and serve.

SmartPoints values per serving 4
SmartPoints values per recipe 17

PUDDINGS

Strawberry & banana sorbet

Serves 2

Prep time
10 minutes
plus freezing

This dessert couldn't be more simple. It looks and tastes amazing and best of all, is zero SmartPoints.

Ingredients
2 bananas
6 large strawberries,
hulled and chopped
1 teaspoon grated
orange zest
Juice of ½ orange

1 Freeze the whole bananas in their skins for 24 hours.

2 Remove the bananas from the freezer and peel. Put them in a food processor or blender, along with the strawberries, orange zest and juice, and process until smooth. Serve immediately or spoon into freezer-safe ramekins and freeze until needed.

SmartPoints values per serving 0
SmartPoints values per recipe 0

Recipe index

SmartPoints index

SmartP●ints weight watchers